FIRSTSTEPSIN CLASSICALPIANO

Learn to Play Classical Piano for Beginners

VANESSA**RICHARDS**

FUNDAMENTAL**CHANGES**

First Steps in Classical Piano

Learn to Play Classical Piano for Beginners

www.fundamental-changes.com

Twitter: **@guitar_joseph**

Over 10,000 fans on Facebook: **FundamentalChangesInGuitar**

Instagram: **FundamentalChanges**

Cover Image Copyright: Shutterstock / Alenavlad

Contents

Introduction

Playing music is a most rewarding activity, whichever instrument you choose. This book aims to show you the basics of piano playing whilst introducing you to well-known pieces from the classical repertoire. The term *classical* in this book does not only refer to the Classical Period of music (which encompasses Beethoven, Mozart and Haydn) but includes music from the Baroque to Romantic periods. In this book you will encounter pieces of music ranging from Bach to Debussy.

This book can be used as a standalone guide to the basics of piano playing, but it is always advisable to work alongside a piano teacher. A teacher can pass on valuable insights and extend your thinking beyond this book. Choose your teacher with care, however, to ensure you get the best opportunities and guidance (see thoughts on choosing a teacher on my website: **https://www.musicinbeverley.com/choosing-a-teacher**)

Playing any instrument requires effort and sustained practice. Our muscles need to be taught new and often intricate movements and this can only be attained with diligence and patience. Muscle memory is the act of an automatic action of muscles which does not need to be thought about. Take the example of walking. We know exactly which muscles need to move for this activity and we don't need to consider them before we walk. In the same way, muscle memory can be developed when learning to play the piano, but it is not automatic – it requires time and practice. This does not need to be long periods of practice. Small and often is generally the best way. 15 to 20 minutes per day is a good amount to aim for when first beginning to play.

As you work through this book, you will find that finger numbers for notes are given in the very first chapter, but not in subsequent chapters (apart from Chapter Six: Accidentals). The reason for this is that all players differ in their approach and finger positions are often a matter of personal preference. As you work through the book you will find which finger positions are most appropriate for you. If you work alongside a piano teacher, discuss and explore these together. Feel free to write your chosen finger positions above the music in pencil.

Metronome markings

Metronome markings indicate the speed of a piece of music. The audio examples in this book are played at 100 crotchet beats per minute unless otherwise stated. However, the metronome markings are only a guide to the speed. All the pieces can be played at a tempo that is comfortable for you.

Most digital pianos include a metronome as standard. If you are using an instrument with no metronome, I suggest you either buy a standard metronome from a music store, or download one of the many metronome apps available for smartphones and tablets.

Get the Audio

The audio files for this book are available to download for free from **www.fundamental-changes.com.** The link is in the top right-hand corner. Simply select this book title from the drop-down menu and follow the instructions to get the audio.

We recommend that you download the files directly to your computer, not to your tablet, and extract them there before adding them to your media library. You can then put them on your tablet, iPod or burn them to CD. On the download page there is a help PDF and we also provide technical support via the contact form.

Twitter: **@guitar_joseph**

Over 10,000 fans on Facebook: **FundamentalChangesInGuitar**

Instagram: **FundamentalChanges**

Chapter One – Navigating the Keyboard

Posture

Before beginning to play the piano it is important to have the correct playing posture. Relax your body by standing away from the keyboard, letting your hands fall loosely to your side. It is advisable to purchase an adjustable stool, to ensure your playing position is relaxed and you are seated at a comfortable height. When seated, lay both hands on the keys with your hands curved. The natural curve of the hand should be maintained whilst playing. Your forearms should be straight and without tension. The illustration below shows the correct seating and hand position.

The piano keyboard is comprised of 88 keys arranged in patterns of white and black notes as shown below.

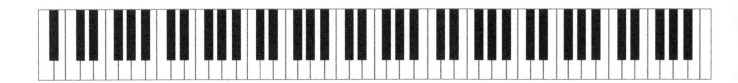

The black keys are arranged in groups of two and three. The white notes are grouped in the order of the musical alphabet: A, B, C, D, E, F, G. The following diagram shows the white notes which make up the musical alphabet.

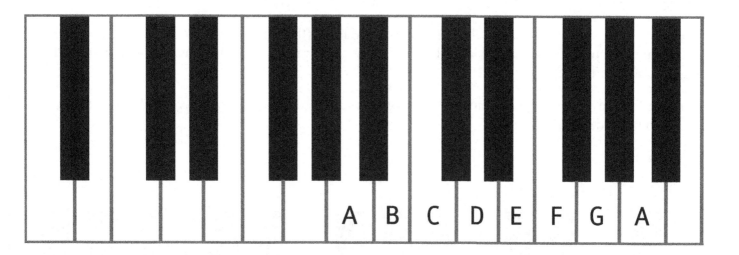

Finger Numbers

To be able to play music on the keyboard it is important to know which fingers to use. Each finger is given a number: 1, 2, 3, 4, 5. The following example shows the finger numbers on each hand with the thumb being finger 1.

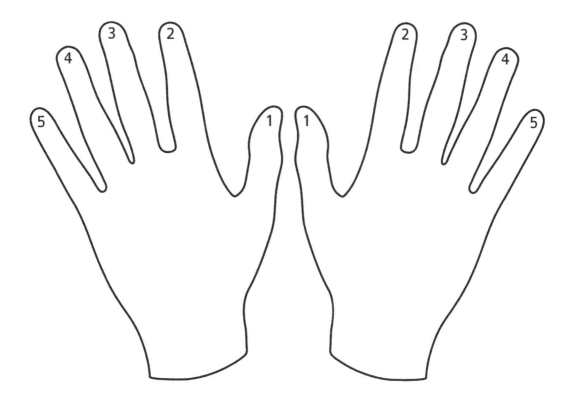

Right Hand Position

The next section shows how the right hand should be positioned in order to play notes from the C Major scale. C Major can be played on piano using only white keys and many pieces of music have been written in C Major, making it an easy key in which to begin your exploration of classical music.

Place your right hand with the thumb (finger 1) on Middle C (the C nearest to the middle of the keyboard). Without moving position, you are able to play the following four notes: D with finger 2, E with finger 3, F with finger 4 and G with finger 5.

Example 1a below shows the placement of the right hand in order to play the micro-scale (a small part of a scale) from Middle C to G.

Example 1a:

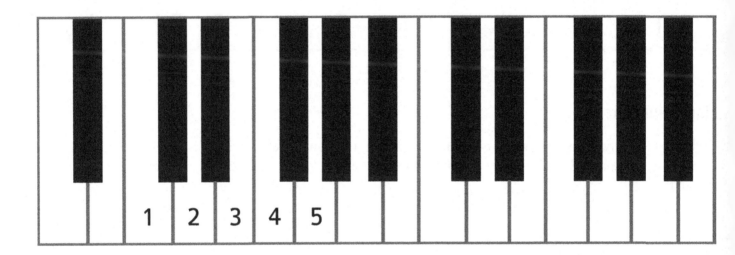

The following extract is the beginning of the Christmas carol *Unto us a Child is Born*, a tune of unknown origin, first seen in a manuscript dating from the 15th Century. This theme uses the notes of the microscale shown in Example 1a. The finger numbers are given above the notes:

Example 1b:

1 2 3 4 43 2 1

C D E F E D C_

The long line after the final C indicates that you should play a longer note.

C Major Scale

Now we will extend the range of notes to cover the full C Major scale. This distance is known as an octave and contains the white notes from Middle C to the next C (referred to as C') in your right hand. By knowing these notes, the range of music you can play is extended.

To play the C Major scale, place your hand as before, with finger 1 (thumb) on Middle C. Play each note in sequence until you get to E, finger 3. Now bring your thumb *under* finger 3 and move your whole hand to the new position and play note F with finger 1 (thumb). Now continue with finger 2 playing G, finger 3 on A, finger 4 on B and finger 5 finishing the scale on C'. **Example 1c** below shows the finger pattern.

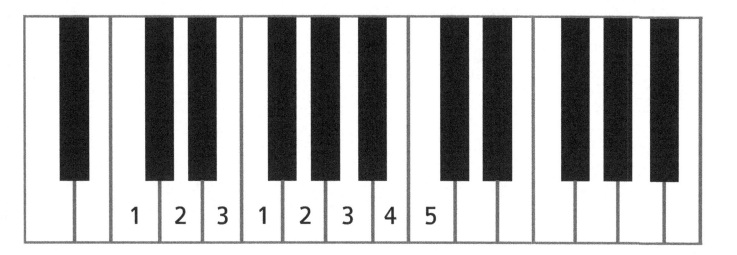

The audio example shows the C Major scale covering one octave from C to C' in the right hand, both ascending and descending. Practise this several times to familiarise yourself with the scale. Try playing the scale at different speeds and with different dynamics (from soft to loud).

This finger pattern for C Major 1, 2, 3, 1, 2, 3, 4, 5 can be continued up the keyboard, playing higher notes. Listen to the audio **Example 1d** to hear how this sounds.

Example 1e is the beginning of perhaps the most famous of all classical pieces: *Symphony No. 5. Op 67. 1st Mov.* by Ludwig van Beethoven. The notes are given below with appropriate finger numbers shown above.

5 5 5 3   4 4 4 2

A A A F___ G G G E___

Example 1f below is an extract from a composition called *La Fille Aux Cheveux De Lin* (The Girl with the Flaxen Hair) by Claude Debussy. It is the eighth piece from his First Book of Preludes. The notes are shown below with the suggested fingering above each note:

5   4 2 1 2 4 5   4 2 1   3 5 3   3 1 4   3 2 1

C'___   AFD_FAC'_AFD_FAF_FDF_EDC___

Note that your fingers do not always remain on the same notes. Listen to Example 1f first, then play along with it. Once you are comfortable with that, play it without the music. The aim is to become familiar with changing finger positions.

Chapter Two – The Musical Stave

In Chapter One we learnt how to navigate the keyboard and play the C Major scale with the right hand. In this chapter we will look at how music is written.

Piano music uses two staves. Each stave has a set of five lines. The staves are connected by a brace at the beginning of the two lines as shown in the diagram below.

Right Hand

The right hand plays the *upper stave* and the left hand plays the *lower stave*. At the beginning of each stave there is a sign to show whether the music is in the treble register (higher register played with the right hand) or the bass register (lower register played with the left hand). These are called the *treble clef* and the *bass clef* and are shown below.

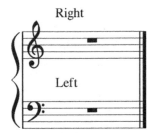

The Musical Alphabet on the Stave

The following diagram shows the keyboard layout and the position of notes on the stave. Note the position of Middle C on the bass stave. If written on the treble stave it would show as a note with a line through it, but with a stem extending upwards.

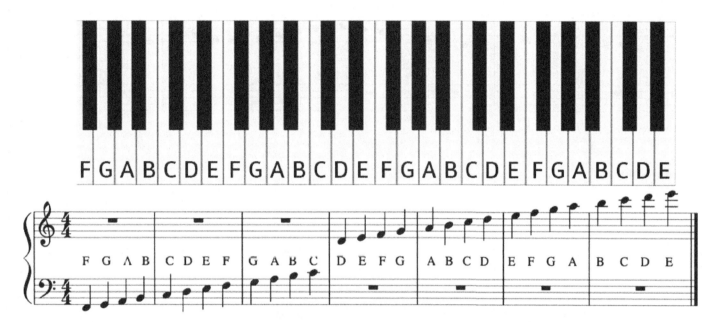

With your right hand, play Middle C with any finger and continue to play ascending notes, naming each as you go until you reach the highest note. These are all notes in the treble clef range.

Play the extract from *Symphony No. 5. Op 67. 1st Mov.* by Ludwig van Beethoven that you learnt in Chapter One starting on any A in the treble octave.

Now play the extract from Debussy's *Le Fille Aux Cheveux De Lin* starting on the highest C in the treble range.

Left Hand

With the left hand play Middle C with any finger and continue playing descending notes, naming each as you go, until you reach the lowest note. These are all notes in the bass clef range.

Warm-Up Activities

It is advisable to warm up prior to playing the piano. To avoid injury, ensure that you never play the piano with cold hands. Throughout this book you will find suggested warm-up activities comprising techniques that have been covered elsewhere. Any combination of these may be used prior to playing.

Using the diagram above to help you read the notes on the stave, work through the examples below. These will form the basis of some warm-up exercises that you can use from now on. The first two examples use the C Major scale for both right and left hands. Play them slowly and evenly with a moderately soft attack to ensure even movement of fingers. You will notice that on the stave where there are no notes, there is a small symbol showing that the bar is empty. This symbol denotes either a full bar rest or 4 beats rest. An audio example is given for each exercise.

Example 2a:

Example 2b:

The next example is based on the two-note pattern taken from *Symphony No 5. Op 67. 1st Mov.* by Ludwig van Beethoven. It uses the notes of the C Major scale. The notes used are arranged in intervals of a third. This simply means that you skip certain notes. In this instance, the first note is played, the second is not played, then the third note is played, and so on.

Example 2c:

Example 2d:

The warm-up exercises can be repeated using a variety of tempi (speeds) and dynamics if desired.

In Chapter One we played the opening theme from *Symphony No. 5. Op 67. 1st mov.* by Ludwig van Beethoven. **Example 2e** shows this theme written on the treble stave (right hand). Notice that there are three notes in this piece that look different from the ones we've encountered so far. I will explain these in more detail in Chapter Three. For now, it's enough to understand that notes with a black base and a stem are *short notes*, and notes with a white base and a stem are longer notes. Notes linked together with a curved line are the longest in length.

Play this melody following the notes on the treble stave. Remember to play for a longer time on the F (finger 3) and the E (finger 2). Listen to **Example 1e** again if a reminder of the tune is needed. Note the symbol at the end of the music denoting a rest.

Example 2e:

Now listen again to *La Fille Aux Cheveux De Lin* (The Girl with the Flaxen Hair) by Debussy. **Example 2f** below shows the tune written on the treble (right hand) stave.

Example 2f:

More Melodies on the Musical Stave

The following examples show some more familiar tunes to play that use only the notes of the C Major scale in the right hand. The right hand should be placed with finger 1 on Middle C. **Example 2g** is the beginning of the famous aria *La Donna e Mobile* from the opera *Rigoletto* by Giuseppe Verdi. Listen to where the long and short notes occur.

Example 2g:

Example 2h is an extract from *Symphony No 9. 2nd Mov. "From the New World"* by Antonin Dvorak. In the orchestral version this tune is played by the *Cor Anglais,* a member of the oboe family.

Example 2h:

The final extract given here is not strictly a classical piece of music, but it is a fun one to play and well worth having in your repertoire. Listen to **Example 2i** first and I am sure you will recognise the tune. Finger 1 should be played on the first note, G.

Example 2i:

Now that you've learnt how notes are placed on the stave, you need to know how long each note should be played for, and how the music stave can be subdivided to make reading the notes easier. We will explore this in the next chapter and revisit some of the tunes learnt in Chapters One and Two to increase your repertoire.

Chapter Three – Note Names and Bar Lines

Warm-Up Activities

The first two warm-up activities are based on the descending three note pattern taken from bar 2 of *Symphony No 9. 2nd Mov. "From the New World"* by Antonin Dvorak.

Example 3a:

Example 3b:

The next four exercises are based on elements of Happy Birthday. The first two examples are based on the interval of a fourth taken from the last two notes of bar 2. It is called a fourth because there are four notes; the first note is played, the second and third notes are not played, and the fourth note is played.

Example 3c:

Example 3d:

The following two examples use the interval of a fifth (five notes in total) taken from bar 4 of Happy Birthday.

Example 3e:

Example 3f:

In chapters One and Two we learnt how to navigate the keyboard and locate the scale of C Major on the musical stave. We've also seen how knowing C Major allows us to play a range of tunes.

The musical examples also showed how notes look different according to their length of play. To be able to play a wider variety of tunes it is necessary to know how long each note lasts and how music is subdivided.

Time in music is divided into bars. A bar is a way of dividing notes into segments, depending on how many beats are in each bar. The boundary of each bar is shown by a vertical line. At the end of the music there is a double bar line – two vertical lines that signal the end of the piece.

To let the pianist know how long a note should last, several different *note symbols* are used, each of which represents a specific number of beats.

Crotchet

A crotchet is a one-beat note. The following example shows the C Major scale written in crotchets.

Example 3g

Minim

A minim is a two-beat note. The following example shows the C Major scale written in minim beats.

Example 3h:

Semibreve

A semibreve is a four-beat note. The following example shows the C Major scale written in semibreve notes.

Example 3i

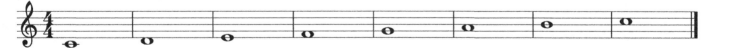

A semibreve can also be used to show a note which lasts a full bar of music. Sometimes bars are not 4 beats in length and we will come to this later in the book. For now, all our bars assume 4 beats in each one.

Bar lengths

Each bar has a specific number of beats within it, shown by two numbers at the beginning of the music. The top number refers to the number of beats, the bottom number to the type of beat. The following diagram shows an example of music that has 4 crotchet beats in each bar. The 4 at the top means 4 beats, the 4 at the bottom means crotchet beats. This is called the *time signature*.

Example 3j shows the C Major scale written on the musical stave using crotchet beats. The 4/4 at the start of the music shows us we have 4 crotchet beats in every bar.

Example 3j

Example 3k is the theme from *Symphony Number 94. 2nd Mov. "Surprise"* by Joseph Haydn. It uses a 4/4 time signature and both crotchet and minim notes. Notice that the crotchet notes have a dot placed below them. This is a *staccato* note.

Staccato

Staccato means to play a note for a shorter time without sustain. To practise this technique, close the piano lid and rest all 10 fingers lightly on top. Lift each finger in turn and press it to the piano lid, releasing it quickly. Now open the lid and try this on the keys. Lift each of your fingers in turn and press each key with a quick finger motion, lifting up from the key swiftly. Note that your arm and hand are hardly moving as the note is depressed and released by your finger.

Example 3k

The theme is in 4/4 so has 4 crotchet beats in each bar. Bars 2, 4, 6 and 8 each have two crotchets and a minim.

More tunes in 4/4

In Chapter Two we played the theme from *Symphony No 9. 2nd Mov. "From the New World"* by Antonin Dvorak. In **Example 3l** we revisit the theme, now written fully on the musical stave. It is in 4/4 time and there are 8 bars. In bars 4 and 8 you can see a semibreve used – a note lasting 4 beats. Unlike the tune played in **Example 3k** this extract is played not staccato, but *legato*.

Legato

Legato is a technique by which notes are played to flow seamlessly from one to another – the opposite of staccato. It enables us to play the piano in a 'singing' style with no detachment between the notes.

The example in **Example 3l** is also played quietly, indicated by the **p** written below the treble stave. **p** is short for *piano*, the Italian word for *quiet*. If the piece was to be played loudly you would see an **f** (short for *forte*, the Italian word for *loud*). These two words describe the full name for the instrument – *pianoforte* – which we usually shorten to 'piano'.

Example 3l

The next tune is an extract from a very well-known piece of music by Jacques Offenbach, *The Can-Can* from *"Orpheus in the Underworld"*. It uses a mixture of crotchet, minim and semibreve notes.

Example 3m

The Sustaining Pedal

The sustaining pedal is the right hand pedal on the piano. The heel of your foot should be in contact with the floor at an angle of about 30 degrees. The pedal is depressed with only a small part of your foot, using your heel as a pivot. Notice that if the pedal is depressed and a note played, the note is sustained even when the pedal is released. When playing with the pedal you will notice the music has a line underneath the bass line, sometimes preceded by *Ped*.

The Ped indication is not always present and sometimes you will see just a line that indicates when to depress the pedal and when to release.

Chapter Four – C Major Left Hand Chord

Warm-Up Exercises

This first warm-up activity is a return to playing C Major in both hands. The scale is to be played in semibreve notes. Listen carefully to the sound of each note and look out for any inconsistency in the dynamic of different notes. The aim is to play the scale smoothly and evenly.

Example 4a:

Example 4b:

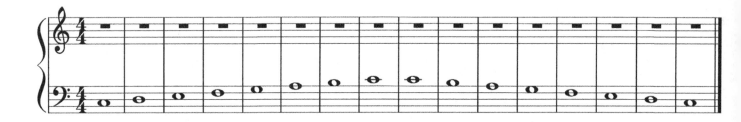

The next two exercises are based on the staccato figure from *Symphony Number 94. 2nd Mov. "Surprise"* by Joseph Haydn. Remember to keep your hands relaxed and use your fingers to create the short staccato notes. The word 'sim' means that the music should be played in a similar manner throughout.

Example 4c:

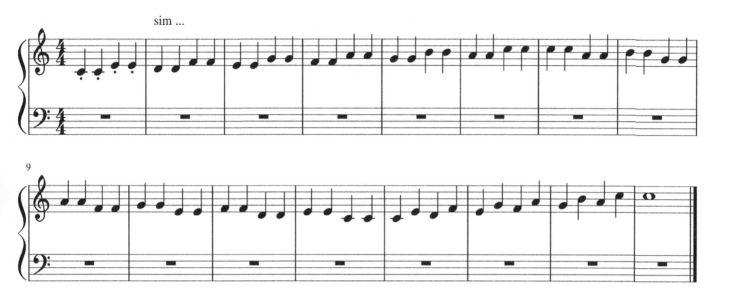

Example 4d:

The final two exercises are based on the penultimate bar from *Symphony No 9. 2nd Mov. "From the New World"* by Antonin Dvorak. This exercise should be played legato – as smooth as possible with no gaps between the notes.

Example 4e:

Example 4f:

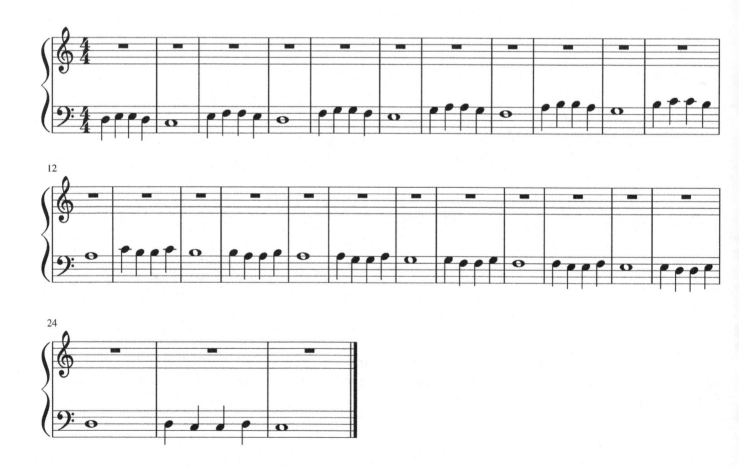

In previous chapters we've played the C Major scale using the right hand. Now the left hand is going to be introduced, allowing an accompaniment to be played to the melodies you are familiar with.

A 'chord' is simply two or more notes played at the same time. Refer back to Chapter Two to revise the position of the notes on the musical stave.

The C Major chord shown below is a simple C Major triad (three notes) comprising C, E and G. These three notes, played together with fingers 5, 3 and 1, form a simple C Major chord. Note that the C Major triad could be played on any C and does not have to start on Middle C.

Example 4g:

This C Major chord can be used to accompany melodies written in C Major. Below is the right hand melody to *Symphony No.9. 2nd Mov. "From the New World"* by Antonin Dvorak that you learnt in Chapter Two (see Example 2h).

Example 2h

The C Major triad is used to harmonise the melody. **Example 4h** shows the melody with the C Major triad adding the harmony. Note that in some bars, only the G of the triad is used. The full triad does not have to be used in order to harmonise a melody.

Example 4h:

Play the same tune, but this time use only the C and G notes in the left hand to accompany it. Notice the difference this small change makes to the whole sound of the music.

Example 4i:

The following melody is an extract from *Symphony No 9, 4th Mov. "Ode To Joy"* by Ludwig van Beethoven. The right hand plays the melody while the left hand plays the accompaniment using the C Major triad. Sometimes the triad is played in full and sometimes only one or two notes are used.

Example 4j:

The final melody we are going to return to is *Symphony No. 94. 2nd Mov. "Surprise"* by Joseph Haydn.

Example 4k:

We've seen how the C Major triad can be used to accompany a melody, and that it's not necessary to play all three notes of the chord all the time. It is also important to know that the notes of the triad can be arranged in a different order to create a different effect. The following examples show different arrangements of the C Major triad beginning with the C,E,G arrangement we learnt in **Example 4g:**

The chord can be played using one or more of the three notes, and the C note does not have to be on the bottom. Playing the same notes but rearranging their order is called a chord inversion. **Example 4l** shows the same three notes, but the sequence is E, G and C.

Example 4l:

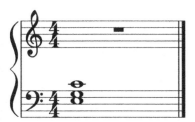

The following example shows the second inversion where G is at the bottom: G, E, C.

Example 4m:

The important thing to remember is that you can play the chord in any order, or with any combination of the three notes. Look back at *Symphony No. 9. 2nd Mov "From the New World"*, by Antonin Dvorak, *Symphony No 94. 2nd Mov. "Surprise"* by Joseph Haydn and *Symphony No. 9. 4th Mov. "Ode To Joy"* by Ludwig van Beethoven. Try playing the melodies as written, but with a different combination of notes in the left hand and hear how this affects the overall sound.

The notes of C Major chord can also be played at different times, rather than simultaneously. This is sometimes called a 'broken chord', as the notes are *broken up* and not played together. The following example uses the major triad C, E, G but broken, so the notes are played one after the other.

Example 4n:

This form of chord is often used in music from the Classical Period, such as that of Haydn and Mozart. A well-known example is shown in the extract below from the first movement of Mozart's *Piano Sonata in C Major K545*. Here, the notes in the left hand are played in a slightly different order: C,G,E,G and so on.

Example 4o:

This specific pattern of notes is well-known technique called an *Alberti Bass*. It works particularly well when the right hand has long notes that do not move quickly. It is well worth finding this musical example online and listening to the pattern in the left hand.

The final piece of music for this chapter is *String Quartet in F major Op3. No 5. Hob. III:17* by Joseph Haydn. This extract is from the second movement entitled *Serenade* which features the Alberti Bass pattern.

Example 4p:

Chapter Five – Two New Time Signatures

Warm-Up Exercises

The first example is an exercise based on the right hand melody from *Symphony No 9, 4th Mov. "Ode To Joy"* by Ludwig van Beethoven. It uses the descending figure in bar 2.

Example 5a:

Example 5b:

In Chapter Four you began to use your left hand as an accompaniment to your right hand, as in this example:

Example 5c:

In Chapter Three, the use of 4/4 as a time signature was introduced. Music, of course, is not always written with 4 crotchet beats in each bar. In this chapter, two new time signatures are introduced: 3/4 and 2/4.

3/4 time signature

A time signature of 3/4 means that the music still counts in crotchet beats, but there are only three in each bar. The example below shows three crotchet beats in the bar on the note A in both right and left hand.

Example 5d:

Minim beats can also still be used in 3/4 time, but as they do not fill a full bar, a crotchet would be used with them.

Example 5e:

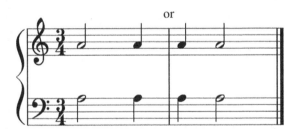

At this point a new note is introduced: *the dotted minim*. A dotted minim is used to signify a note lasting for three beats. In 3/4 time this equals a full bar.

The example below is the C Major scale played in 3/4 time with dotted minim notes.

Example 5f:

You will recognise the sound of 3/4 time from waltzes you've heard. A waltz is a familiar dance in 3/4 time and many classical composers used it. The most well-known are probably those by Strauss (*The Blue Danube*, for instance) and Chopin, who composed a great number of waltzes for piano. It is worth trying to find examples of these.

Example 5g is the theme from the *Waltz of the Flowers* from *"The Nutcracker Suite"* by Tchaikovsky. The left hand has a very common pattern. Here, the three beats are known as the 'oom-pah-pah' figure. It is a version of the left hand C Major chord explained in Chapter Four. This figure is used as a two-bar introduction before the main tune appears in the right hand.

In bars 5 and 6 you can see the same note (E) in both bars joined by a line over the top. This indicates that the two notes are tied together as one long note. The note in bar 6, therefore, does not need to be played so the E will last for 6 beats in total.

Example 5g:

Note the *mp* symbol at the beginning of the music. This is a *dynamic* marking. It provides guidance on the dynamics with which the piece should be played. In this instance, it indicates that it should be played with a moderately quiet dynamic. There are two additional signs: < meaning get gradually louder, and > meaning get gradually quieter. Listen to the audio example to hear how this sounds.

Another dance in 3/4 time is the minuet. This dance is found frequently in the music of Baroque composers such as J. S. Bach and Handel. It continued to be popular well into the Classical Period. The minuet featured below is by Johann Sebastian Bach. It includes a new note: the quaver. Quavers are worth half the length of a crotchet. **Example 5h** shows the C Major scale using quaver beats. Because quaver notes are half the length of crotchets, there are two notes to every beat making the music sound quicker.

Example 5h

This minuet by Johann Sebastian Bach does not have the left hand pattern we saw in the waltz. It was originally written in G Major, but here is it is arranged in C Major.

Example 5i:

The next example is the main theme from *Piano Sonata in G Major Op 49. No. 2* by Ludwig van Beethoven. This is another example of a minuet.

Example 5j

The final time signature we'll look at in this chapter is 2/4. As the numbers signify, there are two crotchet beats in each bar. **Example 5j** below is an *Allegro* by Wolfgang Amadeus Mozart. Allegro simply means *fast*.

Example 5k:

Chapter Six – Accidentals

This chapter doesn't contain any specific warm-up exercises, as many of the examples below will themselves serve as warm-ups.

An *accidental* is a musical symbol indicating a change in pitch. The symbol indicates whether a note is to be raised or lowered by a semitone (one half step), or whether it is to be changed back to its original pitch. The most commonly used are the sharp sign #, the flat sign ♭ and the natural sign ♮.

The Sharp ♯

This sign indicates that a note is to be sharpened by one semitone. On the piano, if we play Middle C it is a white key. If we add a sharp sign ♯ before the note, this raises the note one semitone to C♯. Now it is played on the black key immediately to the right of Middle C. Example 6a shows the position of these two notes on the stave.

Example 6a

The diagram below shows them on the keyboard.

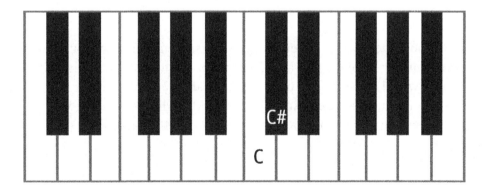

If another C is notated in the same bar, it remains a C♯ unless indicated otherwise. If the note is to revert back to the white C key, then a natural sign ♮ will appear before the note. Look at the example below which shows the notes C and C♯ alternating. Learning to play notes on the black piano keys means that a pianist can extend their repertoire to other pieces of music.

Example 6b:

A common way to practise using sharp keys is to play a *chromatic scale* – a scale that contains every note on the keyboard in a particular order. The example below shows a rising chromatic scale beginning on Middle C in the right hand. Note the ♯ sign in front of certain notes. You will notice that there is no sharp ♯ sign in front of E or B. This is because if you sharpen E it becomes the note F, and if you sharpen B it becomes C. In more complex music, a sharp sign can be used in front of these two notes, but for our purposes it is not necessary.

Each time there is a sharp sign in front of the note it is raised one semitone – one half step to the right (and therefore becomes a black key).

Example 6c:

With the above example, no fingering was given, but using a specific fingering can make the chromatic scale easier to play. Begin with finger 1 (thumb) on Middle C in the right hand, then play C♯ with your 3rd finger, D with 1, D♯ with 3 and E with 1. Because the next note is F, another white note, use finger 2. The pattern can then continue with finger 3 on the black keys and finger 1 on the white keys until you get to the note C at the top, which will be played with finger 2. The diagram below shows the same scale as above, this time with the finger numbers indicated.

The next example gives you the opportunity to try out this pattern with your left hand. The scale begins on the C below Middle C. You may notice that although the pattern remains with finger 1 on white keys and finger 3 on black keys, finger 2 now plays E and B.

Example 6d:

This pattern is useful because it can be replicated across the whole keyboard. This means that you can play every one of the 88 notes using this rising pattern. Start with the lowest note on the keyboard and play every note in turn using this 3, 1 pattern in both hands. Use a metronome at different speeds to play at different tempi.

The Flat ♭

This sign placed before a note indicates the note is to be flattened – lowered one half step to the left.

Placing your left hand with finger 1 (thumb) on Middle C, you will find that if you lower this note a half step, you will play a B (finger 2), so the C is not shown as flattened. We can, however, flatten the B to become B♭ played with finger 3. This is the black key immediately to the left of the white B key.

If we continue the pattern of 3, 1 fingering we explored with sharps, we find that this pattern will still work as it descends: C, B, B♭, A, A♭, G, G♭, F, E, E♭, D, D♭, C.

This is written for the left hand in the example below.

Example 6e:

The following example shows the chromatic scale with flats in the right hand.

Example 6f:

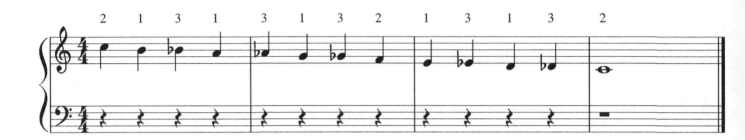

You may have noticed that the black keys can be both flat and sharp depending on the context. For instance, if we flatten the white A key we get A♭ (the black key immediately to the left). If we sharpen the white G key we arrive at G♯, the black key immediately to the right of the G. This is, of course, the same key. A♭ and G♯ are exactly the same note.

The ability to recognise sharps ♯, flats ♭ and naturals ♮ will be useful as we move from C Major to the new keys of G Major and F Major.

In the following examples, you will see how composers have included chromatic figures in their music. The first example is an arrangement of Invitation to the Dance Op 65, J. 260 by Carl Maria von Weber. The Dance is a piano piece that has also been transcribed by Hector Berlioz for orchestra. Note the chromatic figure of G-F♯-G that appears between the rising pattern.

Example 6g:

The next example is the *Crucifixus* from the *Mass in B Minor* by J. S. Bach. The left hand has a beautiful descending chromatic figure underneath the tune. As the music is intended to depict the *Crucifixion* there are some unusual harmonies between the two hands and notes that may seem to clash. The marking *Adagio* indicates it is to be played slowly. The audio example is played at 60 crotchet beats per minute.

Example 6h:

Adagio

Chapter Seven – G Major

Warm-Up Exercises

The first warm-up exercise in this chapter is based upon the *Minuet* by J. S. Bach from Chapter Five. It uses the right hand rising figure and the crescendo featured in bar 1.

Example 7a:

Example 7b:

The next exercise is in 2/4 time, based on the *Allegro* by Wolfgang Amadeus Mozart.

Example 7c:

Example 7d:

The following two exercises are based on the chromatic patterns from Chapter Six.

Example 7e:

Example 7f:

In the previous chapters the melodies learnt were all in C Major and played using only white notes. In order to extend your repertoire, this chapter introduces the key of G Major.

The example below shows the G Major scale on the treble stave. The # sign is placed before the time signature and directly across the F line. This means that all the F notes in this piece are to be sharpened, regardless of their placement on the stave. The F# sharp key is the black key immediately to the right of the F key as explored in Chapter Six. To distinguish the two, remember to look for the sharp ♯ and natural ♮ signs.

Example 7g:

The next example is the G Major scale on the bass stave.

Example 7h:

The following tunes are all in G Major, so watch out for the F#! These melodies are for the right hand only. The first tune is the theme from an Aria from *"The Marriage of Figaro"* by Mozart. An aria is a vocal piece of music, usually part of an opera. Note that the first note is not on the first beat of the bar. It begins on beat 4. This is called a pick-up, upbeat or *anacrusis*.

Example 7i:

The next example is an arrangement of *Dance No 17* from the *Polovtsian Dances* by Alexander Borodin.

Example 7j:

For the final tune we return to a melody played in Chapter Five, the *Minuet* by J. S. Bach. This time it is in its original key of G Major.

Example 7k:

In a similar way to C Major, the left hand can accompany these tunes using a G Major chord. The notes of G Major are G, B and D and can be played in root position, with the G at the bottom.

Example 7l:

The *first inversion* has the B at the bottom.

Example 7m:

The *second inversion* has the D at the bottom.

Example 7n:

As with the C Major chord, the G Major chord can be played in a variety of ways, and with any number of notes. It can be played as a broken chord or as an *Alberti Bass*.

The G Major tunes you've already learnt can now be accompanied with the left hand. Although a left hand part is written in the examples below, you don't have to play them as written. Experiment by playing different arrangements. Each audio example illustrates the written score only.

The Aria from *"The Marriage of Figaro"* by Mozart.

Example 7o:

No. 17 from *"Polovtsian Dances"* by Borodin.

Example 7p:

"Minuet" by J.S. Bach.

Example 7q:

Chapter Eight – Combining C Major and G Major

Warm-Up Exercises

The first warm-up exercise of this chapter reinforces the G Major scale in both hands. The scale can be played at any tempo and with any dynamic to suit, although I advise you to begin slowly.

Example 8a:

Example 8b:

The following three exercises are based on the left hand G Major broken chord. The first example is the chord in root position, the second example is the chord in first inversion, and the final example is the chord in second inversion.

Example 8c:

Example 8d:

Example 8e:

While music is usually assigned a particular key, such as C Major or G Major, chords do not necessarily remain in one key.

For example, you will recall that the notes of the C Major scale are C, D, E, F, G, A and B. The C Major triad consists of C, E and G, and G Major consists of G, B and D. Notice that the notes of the G Major triad are all contained in the C Major scale. If we play a right hand C, we can only play a C Major triad. If, however, we play a right hand G, we can use either a C Major or G Major triad, as G appears in both. In this way music may combine and mix different chords to suit the composer's needs.

In this chapter the pieces all combine both the C Major and G Major triads. The key of the piece (whether it is in C Major or G Major) can be seen by looking at the key signature. C Major has no additional symbols. The key of G Major has a # symbol on the F line of the stave.

The following tune should be familiar to you. It is *The Can Can* from *"Orpheus in the Underworld"* by Offenbach. Whilst it is in C Major, and most of the chords are C Major, the triad of G Major is also used. The first instance is in bar 2 where the right hand plays a D. A triad of C, E, G cannot be played here because it does not contain a D, but the G triad can be used.

The music shows the right hand tune with the name of the chord you should play above. There is no need for a written left hand part – the chord names indicate whether a C or G triad is needed.

Example 8f:

Because the chord symbol does not establish which note of the chord is at the bottom, any of the three notes could be used. Remember that you can also use broken chords or an *Alberti Bass.*

The following examples all have a right hand tune with left hand chords marked above. The first is *"Trumpet Tune"* attributed to Jeremiah Clarke. This is played at 120 beats per minute.

Example 8g:

The next example is the *Waltz* from *"Eugene Onegin"* by Tchaikovsky. This tune introduces a dotted rhythm. A dotted rhythm means that half of the value of the note is added again. For instance, a dotted crotchet is worth 1 crotchet + half of the next crotchet, leaving only 1 quaver at the end. This greats a bouncy feel.

Example 8h:

The following example gives the complete tune with the chord notes written above. As before, the chords can be played in the way that best suits your own style.

Example 8i:

The next example is by Mendelssohn and is entitled *"On Wings of Song"*.

Example 8j:

We complete Chapter Eight with a very well-known tune by Mozart – the theme from the *Clarinet Concert K622. Mov. II.* Bar 8 has no chord symbol and no left hand notes should be played in this bar.

The audio example is played at 80 beats per minute.

Example 8k:

Chapter Nine – F Major

Warm-Up Exercises

The following two exercises are based on the use of the C and G chords. The first warm-up has left hand chord symbols only, while the second includes a right hand melody. Additional warm-up exercises can be taken from any of the previous chapters.

Example 9a:

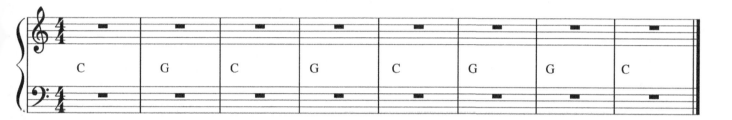

Example 9b:

You have become familiar with the keys and scales of C Major and G Major. In this chapter we will explore F Major. For this key, instead of adding a sharp sign alongside the time signature, we add a flat sign ♭ to the fourth note of the scale. The notes in F Major are F, G, A, B♭, C, D, E and F.

This first example shows the F Major scale on the treble stave.

Example 9c:

The next example is the scale on the bass stave.

Example 9d:

The ♭ sign is placed before the key signature on the B line. This means that all B notes in the piece are to be flattened. The B♭ is the black key immediately to the left of the white B key.

Knowing the scale of F Major will increase your repertoire of tunes still further. Below is a selection of right hand tunes in the key of F Major.

The first example is the well-known Intermezzo Sinfonica from Cavelleria Rusticana by Mascagni. Note the dotted rhythm in bar 2. Listen to the audio example to hear how it's played. The tempo is 80 beats per minute.

Example 9e:

The next piece of music comes from a composer of a much earlier musical period. Handel is most famous for his Water Music and Music for the Royal Fireworks, but this piece is equally as famous. It is the Lascia Ch'io Pianga from "Rinaldo". This example is notated for the right hand. It more difficult than the previous pieces as it has more than one note playing at the same time. The top notes can be played on their own if you wish.

Note that we also have a new rest – a quaver (which looks like the number 7). There are also some points in the music where a B natural ♮ is played. If this is the case, you will see a ♮ before the B note. This symbol, once placed, refers to all notes in that particular bar. It goes back to B♭ in the next bar unless the music says otherwise.

The recording is played at 80 beats per minute.

Example 9f:

As with both the C Major and G Major right hand chords, the left hand F Major chord can be played in a variety of ways. The root chord below shows the position of the notes F, A, C.

Example 9g:

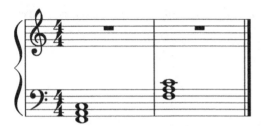

The next example gives the first inversion.

Example 9h:

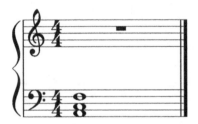

The final example gives the second inversion.

Example 9i

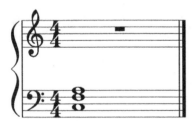

As with the other left hand chords, the notes can be played in any order, and in any time length according to personal taste. Although a left hand part is given in the following examples, it is important to remember that different arrangements can be used, so feel free to experiment.

The example below is an arrangement of the Handel music played above, but this time using both hands. The audio example is played at 80 beats per minute.

Example 9j:

The following music is by Haydn and is a trio taken from *Minuet Number 4* from *24 Minuets*. The right hand has a lovely F Major scale pattern, accompanied in the left by simple F Major chords.

Example 9k:

The concluding piece in this chapter is from *Symphony No. 6 in F Major Op. 68 (Pastoral) Mov. V* by Beethoven. The theme was famously used in the Disney animation *Fantasia*. The recording is played at 120 beats per minute.

Example 9l:

Chapter Ten – Primary Chords in C Major

Warm-Up Exercises

The warm up exercises below are all based in the key of F Major. The rising melody in the first exercise is taken from the Haydn *Minuet*.

Example 10a:

The following exercise is for left hand.

Example 10b:

At this point, you should be fairly familiar with the keys of C, G and F Major. It is useful to know the relationship between these three keys.

In the key of C Major the notes of the scale are C D E F G A B C. To accompany notes in the key of C Major there are three common chords we can use:

  • C Major, which contains the notes C E G.

This is also called by its Roman numeral I as it is the first note of the C Major scale.

  • F Major, which contains the notes F A C.

This is also called by its Roman numeral IV as it is the fourth note of the C Major scale.

  • G Major, which contains the notes G B F.

This is also called by its Roman numeral V as it is the fifth note of the C Major scale.

The left hand normally has a choice of which of the above three chords to play, and any chord that contains the melody note can be used.

  • C can be accompanied by chord I or chord IV as C is in both chords

  • D can *only* be accompanied by chord V as it is the only chord containing a D

  • E can *only* be accompanied by chord I

  • F can *only* be accompanied by chord IV

  • G can be accompanied by chords I or V

  • A can *only* be accompanied by chord IV

  • B can *only* be accompanied by chord V

In the following examples the C Major scale is played with an accompanying left hand figure.

Here it is accompanied by chord I for the C's and chord V for the G's. All chords are in root position i.e. with the first note of the chord at the bottom.

Example 10c:

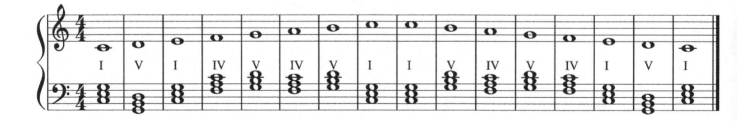

The next example is written with the same chord structure as above, but this time notice the position of the left hand notes. The chords are no longer in the root position, but are arranged so that the voicings of the chord remain smooth as the chords change.

This makes the notes of the left hand closer together and therefore easier to play. Chord inversions are indicated by a small letter after the Roman numeral: **b** indicates a first inversion and c indicates a second inversion. If the chord is in root position no letter is indicated.

Example 10d:

The following example shows the C Major scale with only the chord symbols. This means you can choose the position of the notes yourself. If, for instance, there is a I above the C then the chord played should be C E G. There is no audio example to accompany this exercise.

Example 10e (no audio):

The following example shows the C Major scale played with alternative root position chords. Notice that this example sounds quite different to example 10c.

Example 10f:

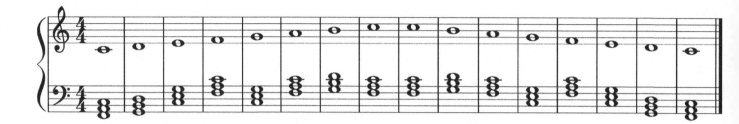

The next example shows the scale played with inversions of left hand chords, and not always in root position.

Example 10g:

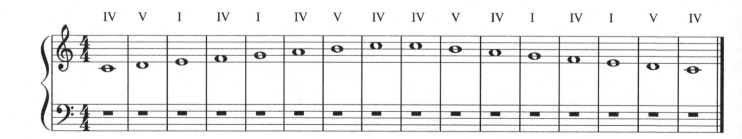

The final example shows the right hand scale with the different Roman numerals given above. This means you can choose your own positions for the chords. There is no audio for this example.

Example 10h (no audio):

The three chords of C, F and G are often referred to as the *primary chords* in C Major.

These chords, I, IV and V, are used in the majority of music in the key of C Major. The following musical examples use a combination of these three chords. The first is an extract from *La Mourisque* by Tylman Susato. In this extract, both Roman numerals and written chords are given. There are no indications of the chord inversions – you can choose what to play. The written left hand is for illustration purposes only.

Example 10i:

The next extract is from a tune written by Charles Dibdin called *Tom Bowling*. Although the title may be unfamiliar, you may well recognise it as the tune played as part of the *Fantasia on British Sea Songs* by Sir Henry Wood during the Last Night of the Proms.

The left hand chords are, again, for illustration purposes only. The audio example is played at 80 beats per minute. *Largo* at the beginning of the piece indicates it should be played with a very slow tempo, usually slower than *Adagio*.

Example 10j:

The final extract given here is the theme from *Trumpet Concerto in E flat Major, Hob. VIIe: Mov 1* by Joseph Haydn. N/C indicates no chord is to be played.

Example 10k:

Chapter Eleven – Music to Enjoy

Congratulations on reaching Chapter Eleven. In the previous chapters we have explored the keys of C Major, G Major and F Major and variety of different notes and time signatures have been covered.

In this chapter a number arrangements of well-known tunes are presented using the three different keys and combinations of the three chords of C Major, G Major and F Major used in the left hand.

C Major

The Blue Danube Waltz by J. Strauss. Chord letters are not given for this piece. The audio example is played at 120 beats per minute.

Example 11a:

Piano Concerto No.15 K545 1st Mov. by Wolfgang Amadeus Mozart. Chord letters are given for this piece should you wish to experiment yourself. The audio example is played at 120 beats per minute.

Example 11b:

F major

Cradle Song by Johannes Brahms. No additional chord numbers or letters are given for this piece. The recording is played at 80 beats per minute.

Example 11c:

Little Serenade by Joseph Haydn. Chord letters are given above the stave, should you wish to experiment yourself.

Example 11d:

G Major

Piano Sonata in G Major Op. 49, No. 2nd Mov. Tempo di Menuetto by Beethoven.

Example 11e:

Ave Verum Corpus from *Requiem in D Major. K618.* The audio example is played at 80 beats per minute.

Example 11f:

Chapter Twelve – Exploring the Keys

This final chapter contains a collection of pieces where the left hand chords are written above the music and no left hand accompaniment is suggested. This gives you the opportunity to experiment with the left hand part. Enjoy the freedom this gives and improvise (make up!) your own accompaniments.

The only audio example is for Example 12d. For all other examples your own improvisations take precedence.

Cradle Song by T. Oesten. This example would work particularly well with broken chords. Where no chord marking is shown, the chord already played remains in place until a new chord is indicated.

The two following examples are extracts from a suite by T. Oesten and the key is C Major. The chords needed, therefore, are

I: CEG

IV: FAC, and

V: GBD.

Example 12a: (no audio)

You will see in the example below that the chords change much quicker than in the previous extract.

Notice the symbol above the rest in bar 13. This is a pause and you may pause the music and restart when ready.

The small triangle above the D in bar 13 indicates the note should be accented (as does the sfz – short for *sforzando*) indication on the last line.

Example 12b: (no audio)

Sonatina No. 1 from Op 36 by Clementi.

Example 12c: (no audio)

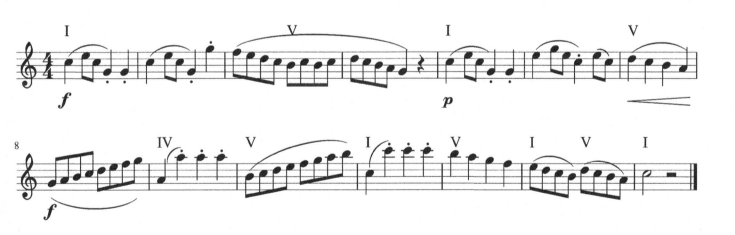

Grande Waltz Brillante. Op 18 by Frederic Chopin. This piece is in a very clear three beat pattern and would benefit from the "oom-pah-pah" pattern discussed in Chapter Five. To achieve this, experiment with playing the root note only on beat 1 of each bar and the other notes of the chord for beats two and three.

Example 12d:

The complete right hand tune with chord symbols is given below.

Example 12e: (no audio)

The final piece returns to a familiar tune, but this time with the accompaniment. Whilst not strictly classical it is a tune well worth having in your repertoire.

Happy Birthday.

Example 12f: (no audio)

Conclusion

Congratulations on successfully mastering *First Steps in Classical Piano*. Taking your first steps on any musical instrument is a challenge, but I hope it has given you an early insight into the world of piano playing. I hope you enjoyed working on some of the best-loved pieces of the classical repertoire.

Playing a musical instrument is a hugely rewarding experience and I trust that you and your teacher are looking forward to exploring further repertoire as you progress. Having worked through the three key signatures presented in this book, you are now ready to consolidate your knowledge of the keys of C, G and F Major and think about the next steps to take you further along your learning journey. I am sure you will enjoy both its challenges and joys. There is a wealth of music out there to suit all players, regardless of level, and I wish you every success in your future endeavours.

About Fundamental Changes

Fundamental Changes is a best-selling music tuition book publishing company with bases close to Manchester and London. Established by author and founder Joseph Alexander, Fundamental Changes aims to provide high quality music tuition across a range of genres. The roots of the comany are in guitar tuition books, but the range is rapidly expanding to include other instruments and vocals.

Find our books on your country's Amazon store. We constantly receive 5-star reviews and our books have been translated into many other languages. For more information visit: **www.fundamental-changes.com**

A Selection of our Titles:

GUITAR

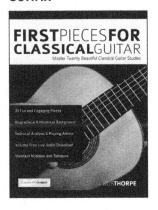

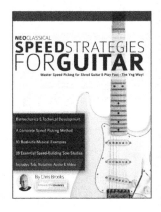

BASS

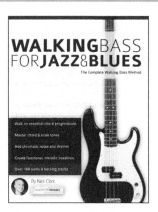

DRUMS

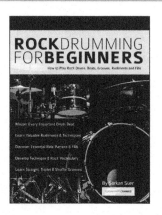
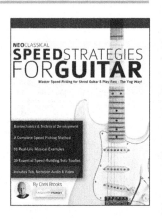

Made in the USA
Monee, IL
23 January 2021